The Ultimate Google Pixel 8 Pro Handbook:

Tips, Tricks, and Tutorials to Make the Most of Your Phone (Complete full guide for beginners and experts)

PATRIK MORAVA

3

Introduction

Imagine a phone that can do everything you want it to do, the phone you've always wanted to make your life easier, better, and more pleasurable. Look no farther than the Pixel 8 Pro if you want a phone that can do it all. The Pixel 8 Pro is the ultimate Google phone, combining the best of Google AI, performance, and design. The Pixel 8 Pro is more than a smartphone; it is your personal assistant, camera, entertainment, and connectivity to the rest of the world.

Design and Innovation

- A gorgeous 6.7-inch OLED display with a refresh rate of 120Hz and a QHD+ resolution, providing sharp and fluid graphics for your photographs, videos, games, and more.

- A powerful Google Tensor G3 chipset that delivers quick and smooth performance, expanded AI capabilities, and a new temperature sensor that can detect ambient temperature and alter the phone's performance accordingly.

- A revolutionary primary camera system comprised of a 50MP main sensor and a 12MP ultra-wide lens capable of capturing stunning images and videos in any lighting condition, with features such as Night Sight, Portrait Mode, Motion images, and more.

- A long-lasting 5000mAh battery that can support up to 30 hours of mixed use and can be swiftly charged using the bundled 30W charger or a compatible wireless charger.

- A sleek and robust design with a curved glass back and a metal frame, IP68 water and dust protection, and a fingerprint sensor on the back for easy and safe unlocking.

- A pure and updated Android experience that operates on the most recent version of Android, which at the time of writing is Android 13, and offers a simple and straightforward interface with new features such as the new design, new privacy settings, new widgets, and more.

- Pixel-exclusive features, like as Call Screen, Now Playing, Live Captioning, and others, that can improve your convenience, entertainment, and accessibility.

- Pixel Watch 2 compatibility, which allows you to connect your Pixel 8 Pro to the Google Pixel Watch 2, a wristwatch powered by Google AI that can provide tailored assistance, safety features, and health insights.

You will learn how to

- set up your Pixel 8 Pro:
- explore its capabilities,
- personalize its settings, and
- troubleshoot common issues in this user guide.

This user guide is aimed for newcomers to the Pixel 8 Pro or Android smartphones in general.

If you are a seasoned user, you may wish to skip some of the parts that discuss the fundamentals.

Chapter 1: Getting started with pixel pro 8

Before you can enjoy all of the features and benefits of your Pixel 8 Pro, you must first perform some fundamental preparations. This section will teach you how to:

- Insert your SIM card into your Pixel 8 Pro to connect to your cell network and make calls, send texts, and utilize mobile Internet.

- Turn on and configure your Pixel 8 Pro so you can activate it, login in to your Google account, transfer data from your old phone, and modify your preferences and security.

- Charge your Pixel 8 Pro so that it is always charged and ready to use.

- Update your Pixel 8 Pro to obtain the most recent software updates and features for your phone.

What's inside the box?

When you purchase a Pixel 8 Pro, you will receive the following accessories in the box:

- The Pixel 8 Pro mobile phone

- The USB-C charger (30W) - The USB-C to USB-C cable

- The SIM tool

Depending on your region and carrier, you may also receive the following items:

- A USB-C to 3.5mm headphone jack adapter

- A USB-C to USB-A converter

- Pixel Buds 2 wireless earphones

If any of these things are missing, please contact your retailer or Google support.

Inserting the SIM card

The SIM card is a tiny chip that is used to identify your phone number and connect you to your mobile network. Before you can make phone calls, send messages, or utilize mobile data, you must first install a SIM card into your Pixel 8 Pro.

Follow these instructions to insert your SIM card into your Pixel 8 Pro:

- Look for the SIM tray near the top of your phone on the left side.

- Gently press the SIM tool or a paper clip into the little hole on the SIM tray until the tray falls out.

- Pull remove the SIM tray and place your SIM card on it, gold contacts facing down and cut-off corner aligned with the tray's notch.

- Replace the SIM tray in the phone until it snaps into place.

- Switch on your phone and wait for it to detect your SIM card.

Depending on the type of SIM card you have, you may need to do the following:

- You can insert a nano-SIM card directly into the SIM tray, as mentioned before.

- If you have a micro-SIM or mini-SIM card, you must use a SIM card cutter or scissors to trim it to the size of a nano-SIM card. Take care not to harm the card's gold contacts or chip. You can also get a new nano-SIM card from your carrier.

- You do not need to insert a physical SIM card into your phone if you have an eSIM card. A digital SIM card that is incorporated in your phone is known as an eSIM card. You can activate your eSIM card by scanning a QR code or inputting your carrier's confirmation code. If you have more than one eSIM card, you can swap between them on your phone.

Turning on and configuring your Pixel 8 Pro

After inserting your SIM card into your Pixel 8 Pro, you must turn it on and set it up so that you can activate it, login in to your Google account, transfer your data from your old phone, and personalize your preferences and security.

Follow these steps to switch on and configure your Pixel 8 Pro:

- Press and hold the power button on your phone's right side until the Google logo displays on the screen.

- Select your language, connect to a Wi-Fi network, and agree to the terms and conditions by following the on-screen instructions.

- If you have an old phone that you wish to transfer your data from, you can use the USB-C to USB-C cable, the USB-C to USB-A adapter, or the Google Backup service to copy your data from your old phone to your Pixel 8 Pro. You can also set up your Pixel 8

Pro as a fresh device, without transferring any data from your old phone.

- Sign in to your Google account, or create one if you don't already have one. Your Google account will get you access to all Google services and apps on your phone, including the Google Assistant, Google Photos, and the Google Play Store. If you like, you can also login in to other accounts, such as your email, social networking, and cloud storage.

- Configure your security settings, such as fingerprint, face unlock, pattern, PIN, or password, to safeguard your phone and data from illegal access. You may also configure the smart lock to keep your phone unlocked while it is close to you, in a trusted location, recognizes your voice, or detects body movement.

- Change the date and time, the wallpaper, the theme, the music, the vibration, the notifications, and the accessibility. You can also enable or disable some features, such as Google Assistant, GPS, Bluetooth, NFC, and dark mode.

- Finish the setup and start enjoying your Pixel 8 Pro.

Charging your Pixel 8 Pro

Your Pixel 8 Pro features a 5000mAh battery that can last up to 30 hours of mixed usage, depending on your settings and usage patterns. You must, however, charge your phone on a regular basis to maintain it fueled and ready to use.

You have two choices for charging your Pixel 8 Pro:

- You may charge your phone via the USB-C port on the bottom of your phone with the included 30W USB-C charger and USB-C to USB-C connection. This is the quickest and most efficient way to charge your phone, since it can charge it from 0% to 50% in just 15 minutes and from 0% to 100% in approximately 90 minutes.

- To charge your phone without using cords, use a suitable wireless charger. This is a quick and easy way to charge your phone because you simply place it on the wireless charger and it begins charging automatically. This is a slower and less efficient method of charging your phone, since it can charge it from 0% to 50% in around 30 minutes and from 0% to 100% in about 180 minutes.

You can check your Pixel 8 Pro's battery level and status by doing the following:

- If your phone is charging, glance at the battery icon in the upper right corner of your screen, which displays the percentage of the battery remaining and the charging status.

- You may open the notification panel by swiping down from the top of your screen and tapping on the battery icon to get more information about your battery usage, battery saver, and adaptive battery.

- To access more information and options about the battery, such as battery usage by app, battery optimization, battery health, and battery suggestions, head to the Settings app and touch on Battery.

Updating Your Pixel 8 Pro

Your Pixel 8 Pro is running the most recent version of Android, Android 13, at the time of writing. However, Google constantly releases software updates for your phone that can improve its performance, security, and functionality. As a result, you should upgrade your phone on a frequent basis if you want to get the most out of it.

You have two choices for updating your Pixel 8 Pro:

- You can wait for automatic updates, which are automatically downloaded and installed on your phone when it is linked to a Wi-Fi network and a power source, as well as when it is inactive. You will be notified when an update is ready and when it is done. To apply the update, you may need to restart your phone.

- You can manually check for and install updates, which are downloaded and installed on your phone when you check for updates and confirm to install the update. You may check for updates by navigating to the Settings app, then selecting System,

Advanced, and System update. To apply the update, you may need to restart your phone.

You have now completed the initial setup procedures for your Pixel 8 Pro. You can now explore the features, modify the settings, and handle issues with your phone, as outlined in the sections below.

Chapter 2

Basic Features of Google pixel 8 pro

You may use your Pixel 8 Pro's basic capabilities to connect with your phone, talk with contacts, capture moments, surf the web, download apps, and more. This section will teach you how to use the following basic features:

- The touchscreen, which is the primary interface for interacting with your phone via motions such as tapping, swiping, pinching, and turning.

- The buttons and ports, which are the actual components of your phone that you may use to switch it on and off, adjust the volume, unlock it, charge it, and insert the SIM card.

- The Google Assistant, a clever and useful tool that can answer questions, conduct tasks, and control your phone and other devices using your voice or a squeeze of your phone.

- The Pixel Launcher, which serves as your phone's home screen and app drawer, allowing you to access your apps, widgets, shortcuts, and alerts.

- Google Camera, your phone's camera app, where you can shoot great photographs and videos with the new primary cameras and advanced features like Night Sight, Portrait Mode, Motion photographs, and more.

- Google images, your phone's photo and video gallery, where you can browse, edit, share, and backup your images and videos with unlimited storage and intelligent features like Memories, Albums, and Printing.

- Google Messages, your phone's messaging software, where you may send and receive text messages, chat messages, stickers, emoticons, and other messages with your friends and groups.

- Google Phone, which is your phone's phone app that allows you to make and receive phone calls, voicemails, and video chats with your contacts and groups.

- Google Chrome, your phone's web browser, where you can browse the web, search the internet, bookmark your favorite websites, and sync your data between devices.

- The Google Play Store, your phone's app store, where you can download and update apps, games, books, movies, music, and other content from Google and other developers.

Using the Touchscreen

The touchscreen is the primary interface for interacting with your phone, and it supports a variety of movements including as tapping, swiping, pinching, and spinning. The touchscreen allows you to navigate your phone, select items, enter text, zoom in and out, and do other things.

To operate the touchscreen, you must first learn the following gestures:

Tap: Use your finger to softly and rapidly tap the screen to pick an item, open an app, confirm an activity, or input a letter on the keyboard.

Double tap: Use your finger to quickly tap the screen twice to zoom in or out on a photo, map, or web page, or to play or pause a video or song.

Long press: Use your finger to touch and hold the screen to access more options for an item, such as opening a menu, relocating an app, or copying text.

Swipe: Slide your finger across the screen to scroll through a list, page, or screen, return to the previous screen, dismiss a notification, or unlock your phone.

Drag: Touch and hold an item on the screen, then drag your finger to move it, for example, rearranging an app, choosing text, or adjusting a slider.

Pinch: Touch the screen with two fingers and move them closer or farther apart to zoom in or out on a photo, map, or web page, resize a widget, or rotate a photo.

Rotate: Place two fingers on the screen and move them in a circular motion to rotate a photo, map, or web page, or to change the orientation of your screen.

Using the Buttons and Ports

The buttons and ports are the actual components of your phone that you may use to switch it on and off, adjust the volume, unlock it, charge it, and insert the SIM card. To use your phone properly, you must understand the placement and function of each button and port.

To utilize the buttons and ports, you must understand the following:

Power button:

The power button is placed near the top of your phone on the right side. You may turn your phone on and off by pushing and holding the power button for a few seconds until the Google logo shows or vanishes on the screen. When your phone is turned on, you may also use the power button to lock and unlock it by pushing it momentarily. You can also reach the power menu by pressing and holding the power button for a few seconds while your phone is turned on, and then selecting choices such as restarting your phone, taking a screenshot, or activating emergency mode.

Volume controls:

The volume controls are on the right side of your phone, just below the power button. You may control the volume of your phone's ringtone, notification sound, media sound, and alarm sound using the volume buttons.

You can also mute or unmute your phone by pressing the volume down button until the volume icon shows a slash, or the volume up button until the volume icon shows a sound wave.

You can also utilize the volume buttons to reach the volume menu while your phone is turned on by pressing either the volume up or volume down button and then selecting from the options such as do not disturb mode, sound mode, or live caption.

Fingerprint sensor:

The fingerprint sensor is positioned towards the top center of your phone's back. When your phone is locked, you can use the fingerprint sensor to unlock it by touching it with your registered finger. When your phone is unlocked, you may also use the fingerprint sensor to access the notification panel by swiping down on the sensor.

When prompted, you can use the fingerprint sensor to authorize payments, sign in to apps, or confirm actions by tapping the sensor with your registered finger. You may register up to five fingerprints on your phone by navigating to the Settings app, pressing on Security, then Pixel Imprint, and following the on-screen steps.

USB-C port:

The USB-C port is positioned in the center of the bottom of your phone. You may charge your phone via the **USB-C** port by connecting it to the supplied *30W USB-C* charger or a compatible wireless charger via the **USB-C** to **USB-C** connection. You can also transfer data using the **USB-C** port by connecting it to a computer or another device with a **USB-C** to **USB-C** cable or a **USB-C** to **USB-A** converter. You can also attach peripherals like as headphones, speakers, or converters to the USB-C port by utilizing the USB-C to 3.5mm headphone adapter or the USB-C to **HDMI** adapter.

SIM tray:

The SIM tray is positioned near the top of your phone on the left side. You can insert the SIM card into your phone by gently pushing into the small hole on the SIM tray with the SIM tool or a paper clip until the tray pops out, then placing your SIM card on the tray with the gold contacts facing down and the cut-off corner aligned with the notch on the tray, and then pushing the tray back into the phone until it clicks into place.

How to Make Use of Google Assistant

The Google Assistant is a clever and useful tool that can answer questions, conduct activities, and manage your phone and other devices using your voice or a squeeze of your phone. You may use Google Assistant to perform the following:

- Check the weather, news, traffic, or sports scores. - Create alarms, timers, reminders, or calendar events.

- Make calls, send messages, or begin video conversations.

- Listen to podcasts, music or watch videos.

- Look for information on the internet, obtain directions, or translate language

- Take photographs, selfies, or videos.

- Launch applications, change settings, or toggle features.

- Manage smart home devices including lights, thermostats, and cameras.

- Have enjoyable chats, play games, and make jokes.

To utilize the Google Assistant on your Pixel 8 Pro, you must have the Google Assistant app loaded on your phone, which comes pre-installed. You'll also need a Google account, which you can get for free if you don't already have one.

Depending on your preferences and convenience, there are several methods to activate the Google Assistant on your Pixel 8

Pro. You can use any of the techniques listed below:

- When your phone is unlocked or on the lock screen, say "OK Google" or "Hey Google," and then ask your query or issue your order. Because you don't have to touch your phone at all, this is the simplest and most convenient method to utilize Google Assistant.

However, you must enable the voice match function on your phone in order for the Google Assistant to identify and respond to your voice.

You may enable the voice match function by opening the Google Assistant app, pressing on the Profile icon, then Assistant settings, then Voice match, and finally following the steps.

- Squeeze your phone's bottom half, then ask your query or give your order. Because you can activate the Google Assistant with a simple motion, this is a novel and entertaining way to utilize it.

However, you must enable your phone's active edge function, which allows you to press your phone to access the Google Assistant.

You may enable the active edge function by navigating to the Settings app, selecting System, Gestures, and Active Edge, and then following the steps.

- Hold down the power button while asking your query or saying your order. Because you can reach the Google Assistant using a familiar button, this is a novel and convenient way to utilize it. However, you must enable the power button function on your phone, which allows you to reach the Google assistant by pressing and holding the power button. You may enable the power button option by navigating to the Settings app, selecting System, Gestures, and Hold for Assistant, and then following the instructions.

- Swipe up from the bottom left or right corner of your screen, then ask your inquiry or command. Because you can reach the Google Assistant with a simple swipe, this is an alternate and convenient method to use it.

To use the Google Assistant, you must first enable the corner swipe function on your phone, which allows you to swipe up from the bottom corners of your screen.

You can enable the corner swipe function by opening the Settings app, heading to System, Gestures, Swipe to launch Assistant, and following the instructions.

- On the home screen or in the app drawer, tap the Google Assistant icon, then ask your inquiry or utter your command. Because you can access the Google assistant with a single swipe, this is a quick and easy method to use it.

However, you must have the Google assistant symbol on your phone in order to activate the Google assistant app with a single press.

You may add the Google Assistant symbol to your phone by opening the Google Assistant app, pressing on the Profile icon, then Assistant settings, Phone, then Add Google Assistant to home screen.

How to Use the Google Pixel Launcher.

The Pixel Launcher is the home screen and app drawer for your Pixel 8 Pro, from which you can access your apps, widgets, shortcuts, and alarms.

The Pixel Launcher is designed to deliver a simple and uncomplicated experience, with features like as the Google search button, Google Assistant, the At a Glance widget, adjustable icons, and app suggestions.

To use the Pixel Launcher, you must first understand:

How to Access the Home Screen, the App Drawer, and the Google App.

How to Add, Remove, and Rearrange Apps and Widgets on the Home Screen.

How to Modify the Home Screen Preferences and Settings.

Shortcuts & Features in Pixel Launcher.

How to Access the Home Screen, the App Drawer, and the Google App.

The home screen is your Pixel 8 Pro's main screen, and it displays your wallpaper, programs, widgets, and shortcuts. You may have many home screens and alternate between them by swiping left or right.

The app drawer alphabetically lists all of the apps installed on your Pixel 8 Pro.

Slide up from the bottom of the home screen to open the app drawer, then swipe down to close it. Slide up to see more applications and down to see fewer apps in the app drawer.

The Google app shows your Google feed, which includes personalized and relevant information such as weather, news, traffic, and sports scores.

Swipe right from the left-most home screen to enter the Google app, and slide left to quit it. You may also launch the Google app by touching the Google logo in the upper left corner of your home screen.

How to Add, Remove, and Rearrange Apps and Widgets on the Home Screen

You may customize your home screen by adding, removing, and rearranging the programs and widgets you use frequently or want quick access to.

To add an app or a widget to the home screen, follow these steps:

To reach the app drawer, swipe up from the bottom of the home screen.
Locate and hold the app or widget you want to add.

Drag the app or widget to an empty area on the home screen and release it.
If you want to add a widget, you may need to select its size and style before selecting Add widget.

To remove an app or a widget from the home screen, follow these steps:

Hold down the app or widget you want to remove until it vibrates.

Drag the app or widget to the Remove icon at the top of the screen to uninstall it.

To rearrange an app or a widget on the home screen, follow these steps:

Hold down the app or widget you want to move until it vibrates.

Drag the app or widget to a new spot on the home screen and release it.

How to Modify the Home Screen Preferences and Settings

By entering the home screen menu, you may change the wallpaper, theme, icons, grid size, and other home screen settings and preferences.

To access the home screen menu, perform the following steps:

To access the menu, tap and hold an empty place on the home screen.

Tap the desired function, such as Wallpaper, Styles & wallpapers, Home settings, or Widgets.

To change the wallpaper, follow these steps:

Select Wallpaper from the home screen menu.

Choose a wallpaper from a category, such as Live wallpapers, My photos, or Art & culture, or tap Explore more wallpapers to see what more the Google Wallpapers app has to offer.

Tap on the wallpaper you want to use to have it appear on your home and lock screens.

Set the wallpaper and choose whether it should display on the home screen, the lock screen, or both.

To change the theme, perform the following steps:

Select Styles & Wallpapers from the home screen menu.

Choose from one of the available themes, such as Crayon, Ash, or Collage, or hit Custom to make your own.

If you select Custom, you may then customize your theme's font, icon shape, accent color, and icon pack before selecting Next.

Give your theme a name and then press the Apply button.

To replace the icons, perform the following steps:

Select Home settings from the home screen menu.

Tap on Icon pack to select an icon pack from the selection, such as System, Pixel, or Lawnicons.

To see the icons on your home screen and app drawer change, tap Apply.

To change the size of the grid, perform the following:

Select Home settings from the home screen menu.

Select a grid size from the drop-down menu, such as 5x5, 4x4, or 3x3, by tapping Grid size.

Tap Apply to see the grid size change on your home screen and app drawer.

Shortcuts & Features in Pixel Launcher

The Google search button, Google Assistant, the At a Glance widget, adjustable icons, and app suggestions are just a few of the features and conveniences available in the Pixel Launcher that may boost your productivity and convenience.

To use the Google search button, follow these steps:

Tap the Google icon in the upper left corner of the home screen to open the Google search bar, where you may search the web or your smartphone with your voice or keyboard.

Tap the microphone icon to the right of the search bar to use your voice to search the web or your device, or to ask the Google Assistant a question or a command.

To use Google Lens, tap the Lens icon to the left of the search bar to scan objects, messages, or codes with your camera and receive information or actions in return.

To use the Google Assistant, perform the following steps:

When your phone is unlocked or on the lock screen, say "OK Google" or "Hey Google," followed by your question or request. As mentioned in the last section, make sure your phone's voice match feature is turned on.

Squeeze the bottom half of your phone, then ask your question or provide your order. Make sure the active edge function is enabled on your phone by going to the Settings app, selecting System, then Gestures, then Active Edge, and following the on-screen instructions.

While asking your question or giving your order, hold down the power button.

Make sure your phone's power button feature is enabled by going to the Settings app, selecting System, then Gestures, then Hold for Assistant, and following the instructions.

Swipe up from the bottom left or right corner of your screen and enter your question or command.

Check that your phone's corner swipe capability is enabled by going to the Settings app, selecting System, then Gestures, then Swipe to Launch Assistant, and following the steps.

On the home screen or app drawer, tap the Google Assistant icon, then type your inquiry or command.

Navigate to the Google Assistant app, tap the Profile icon, then Assistant settings, Phone, then Add Google Assistant to home screen.

To use the At a Glance widget, follow these steps:

Look at the At a Glance widget at the top of the home screen to see the current date, time, weather, and upcoming activities or reminders.

Tap on a date or time to open the Calendar app, where you can check your calendar and add, delete, or amend events and reminders.

Tap the weather symbol to open the Weather app, where you can see the current conditions, hourly forecast, and daily forecast for your location and other locations.

Tap on the event or reminder to see additional information, make changes, or cancel the event or reminder.

To utilize the customizable icons, follow these steps:

Look for customizable icons on your home screen and app drawer that change shape and color depending on your theme and wallpaper.

Tap on the icons to access the apps as normal.

Long-press the icons to get app shortcuts, which are fast operations associated with the apps, such as sending a message, taking a photo, or playing a playlist.

To use the app suggestions, follow these steps:

Swipe up from the bottom of the home screen to open the app drawer and view the app suggestions, which are five apps that the

Pixel Launcher thinks you'd be interested in based on your usage history and context.

Tap on the app suggestions as normal to access the applications.

Long press on the app suggestions to get the app shortcuts mentioned above.

Swipe left or right to reject app suggestions if you do not want to use them.

How to Make Use of the Google Camera

The Google Camera app on your Pixel 8 Pro allows you to shoot great photographs and movies using the new primary cameras and sophisticated capabilities such as Night Sight, Portrait Mode, Motion photographs, and more.

The Google Camera is meant to offer you the best results possible with the least amount of work and settings by utilizing Google AI and the Google Tensor G3 processor.

To utilize the Google Camera, you must first learn the following:

How to open the Google Camera:

You can open the Google Camera by tapping on the Camera icon on the home screen or app drawer, or by double-pressing the power button, or by saying "OK Google, take a photo" or "OK Google, take a video" to the

Google Assistant, or by squeezing the bottom half of your phone and saying "take a photo" or "take a video" to the Google Assistant.

How to change camera modes

You can change camera modes by swiping left or right on the viewfinder or by touching on the mode icons at the bottom of the viewfinder. The camera modes are as follows:

Camera:

The default mode, in which you may capture images with either the primary camera or the ultra-wide camera by pressing the shutter button.

You may also zoom in and out by squeezing the viewfinder or touching on the zoom symbols at the bottom.

More choices, including as the flash, timer, motion, ratio, and settings, may be accessed by touching on the arrow symbol at the top of the viewfinder.

Video:

This is the mode in which you may capture videos with either the main camera or the ultra-wide camera by pressing the record button. You may also zoom in and out by squeezing the viewfinder or touching on the zoom symbols at the bottom.

You may also access other choices, such as the flash, stabilization, resolution, and settings, by pressing on the arrow symbol at the top of the viewfinder.

Portrait:

This is the mode in which you may snap images with a blurred backdrop by touching the shutter button.

You may also zoom in and out by squeezing the viewfinder or touching on the zoom symbols at the bottom.

You may also access extra choices, such as the flash, timer, face retouching, and settings, by pressing on the arrow symbol at the top of the viewfinder.

Night Sight:

This is a setting that allows you to capture images in low-light circumstances simply touching the shutter button.

You may also zoom in and out by squeezing the viewfinder or touching on the zoom symbols at the bottom.

You may also access other choices, including as the flash, timer, focus, exposure, and settings, by touching on the arrow symbol at the top of the viewfinder.

You can also utilize the Night Sight mode to shoot images of the stars by pressing on the *Astrophotography* icon at the top of the viewfinder and setting your phone on a sturdy surface while waiting for the exposure to finish.

Panorama:

This mode allows you to shoot images of a large scene by hitting the shutter button and moving your phone slowly and steadily in one direction while following the arrow in the viewfinder.

You may also select a panoramic type by pressing on the icon at the bottom of the viewfinder, which includes horizontal, vertical, and wide-angle panoramas.

Photo Sphere:

This mode allows you to photograph a 360-degree scene by pressing the shutter button and rotating your phone to align the dots on the viewfinder until the circle is complete.

You can also view your photo sphere by moving your phone about or swiping on the screen after hitting the preview symbol in the lower right corner of the viewfinder.

Slow Motion:

By touching on the record button, you may record videos in slow motion.

You may also select the slow motion speed by touching on the symbol at the bottom of the viewfinder, *such as 1/4x, 1/8x, or 1/16x.*

You can also modify your slow motion movie by pressing on the preview button in the bottom right corner of the viewfinder and adjusting the start and finish points of the slow motion effect using the sliders on the timeline.

Time Lapse:

This mode allows you to capture videos in rapid succession by hitting the record button.

You can also change the pace of the time lapse by touching on the symbol at the bottom of the viewfinder, which allows you to choose between *5x, 10x, or 30x.*

You can also modify your time lapse movie by pressing on the preview button in the bottom right corner of the viewfinder and adjusting the start and finish points with the sliders on the timeline.

Switching between cameras:

You can switch between the primary camera and the ultra-wide camera by touching on the camera symbols at the top of the viewfinder or swiping up and down on the viewfinder.

You can also switch between the rear camera and the front camera by double-twisting your phone, saying "OK Google, switch camera" to the Google Assistant, or squeezing the bottom half of your phone and saying "switch camera."

View and edit your photographs and videos:

To view and edit your images and videos, tap on the preview symbol in the bottom right corner of the viewfinder, or launch the Google photographs app on your phone.

You may also share and backup your photographs and videos by pressing the share or backup icons at the top of the screen, or by using the Google photographs app on your phone.

How to Make Use of Google Photos

Google Photos is your Pixel 8 Pro's picture and video gallery, where you can browse, edit, share, and backup your photos and videos with unlimited storage and smart features like Memories, Albums, and Printing.

Google Photos is more than just a gallery; it is your own picture assistant, capable of organizing, enhancing, and reliving your memories with the power of Google AI.

To utilize Google Photos, you must first learn the following:

How to launch Google Photos:

To open Google Photos, touch on the Photos icon on the home screen or in the app drawer, or say "OK Google, open Photos" to the Google Assistant, or squeeze the bottom half of your phone and say "open Photos."

Viewing your photographs and movies:

You may browse your photos and videos by scrolling through the main screen of Google photographs, where they are grouped by date, from most recent to oldest.

You may also see your photographs and videos by pressing on the Search icon at the bottom of the page, where you'll find them organized into categories like People, Places, Things, Types, and Favorites.

You may also see your images and movies by pressing on the Library button at the bottom of the screen, where you'll find them grouped into albums like Camera, Screenshots, Movies, and Archive.

You can also browse your images and videos by pressing on the For You button at the bottom of the page, where you can see Google images-curated photos and videos, such as Memories, Creations, and Suggestions.

How to edit your pictures and videos:

To edit your photos and videos, touch on the photo or video you want to edit, then tap on the Edit icon at the bottom of the screen to access numerous editing options such as

Filters, Adjust, Crop, Rotate, Markup, and Export.

You may also edit your photographs and videos by touching on the image or video you wish to modify and then swiping up on the screen to get other options like Info, Delete, Archive, and Print.

You can also edit your images and videos by touching on the photo or video you wish to edit, then tapping on the More button in the upper right corner of the screen, where you can access further options like as Share, Save to device, Use as, and Slideshow.

How to share your photos and videos:

To share your photos and videos, tap on the photo or video you want to share, then tap on the Share icon at the bottom of the screen, where you can select the app, contact, or method to share with, such as Messages, Email, WhatsApp, Facebook, or Link.

You can also share your photos and videos by tapping on the photo or video you want to share, then tapping on the More icon in the top right corner of the screen, where you can select the option to share with, such as Create album, Create movie, Create collage, or Create animation.

You may also share your photographs and videos by tapping on the photo or video you want to share, then sliding up on the screen to select the option you want to share with, such as Print, Order photo book, or Order canvas print.

How to create your album on Google photo.

- On your phone, use the Google Photos app and, if necessary, check in to your Google account.

- At the bottom, touch Library, then Albums.

- Tap Create album in the upper right corner, followed by Select photographs.

- Select the photographs and videos you wish to include in your album, then press Add.

- You may also give your album a title and make changes to it as you see fit.

- To share your album with others, touch Share and select the appropriate option.

How to backup your pictures and videos:

To backup your photos and videos, enable the backup and sync function in Google pictures, which allows you to upload your photos and videos to your Google account and view them from any device, with limitless storage and great quality.

You can enable backup and sync by opening the Google Photos app, clicking on the Profile symbol in the upper right corner of the screen, then Photos settings, Backup and sync, and sliding the switch to the on position.

By tapping on the options beneath the Backup and sync menu, you can also adjust backup parameters such as upload size, cellular data use, backup device folders, and backup account.

How to Make Use of Google Messages

Google Messages is your Pixel 8 Pro's messaging software, where you may send and receive text messages, chat messages, stickers, emoticons, and other communications with your friends and groups. With the power of Google AI and the Google RCS, Google Messages is more than just a messaging app; it is your own communication center that can help you stay in contact, express yourself, and have fun.

To utilize Google Messages, you must first learn the following:

How to launch Google Messages:

launch Google Messages by pressing on the Messages icon on the home screen or app drawer, or by saying "OK Google, open Messages" to the Google Assistant, or by squeezing the bottom half of your phone and saying "open Messages."

How to Start a discussion:

You may start a discussion by pressing on the Start chat icon in the bottom right corner of the screen, then selecting the contact or group with whom you wish to communicate, or by entering the recipient's phone number or email address.

You may also start a discussion by tapping on the contact or group with whom you wish to communicate from the list of your recent interactions on the Google Messages home screen.

Sending a message:

To send a message, type your message in the message box at the bottom of the screen and then hit the Send icon.

You may also use your voice to send a message by touching on the Microphone button and then delivering your message.

You may also use the Google Assistant to send a message by clicking on the Google Assistant icon and then asking the Google Assistant to do so, such as "OK Google, send a message to Jude saying I'm on my way."

How to send a chat message:

You may send a chat message by utilizing Google RCS, which is a new messaging protocol that adds extra capabilities to ordinary text messages, such as read receipts, typing indications, high-quality media, and group chat administration.

You may send a chat message using the same methods as a text message, but the message box and message bubble will display a Chat icon instead of a Send symbol, and a Chat label instead of a Text message label.

You may also use the Google Assistant to send a chat message by requesting the Google Assistant to do so, such as "OK Google, send a chat message to Jude saying I'm on my way."

You may only send a chat message to a contact or group that supports Google RCS; otherwise, your message will be delivered as a text message.

If a contact or a group supports the Google RCS, the message box will display "Chat message" or "Text message," depending on the availability of the Google RCS.

You may also enable or disable Google RCS by opening the Google Messages app, clicking the More symbol in the upper right corner of the screen, then Settings, Chat features, and sliding the switch next to Enable chat features.

How to Send a Sticker:

To send a sticker, touch on the Sticker symbol at the bottom of the screen and then select the sticker from the list of available stickers.

You can also download new stickers by pressing on the Add icon and then selecting the sticker pack from the Google Play Store.

You may also send a sticker by asking the Google Assistant to send one, for example, "OK Google, send a sticker to Jude saying I'm happy."

Sending an emoji:

You may send an emoji by pressing on the Emoji symbol at the bottom of the screen and then selecting the emoji from the list of available emojis. You can also get more emojis by pressing on the Category icons and then selecting a category, such as Smileys, Animals, Food, or Flags.

You may also send an emoji by asking the Google Assistant to send one, for example, "OK Google, send an emoji to Jude, saying I'm sad."

Sending a snapshot or video:

You may transmit a photo or a video by pressing on the Camera symbol at the bottom of the screen, then selecting the photo or video from the list of your recent photographs and videos, or by shooting a new photo or video by tapping on the Shutter icon.

You may also modify your photo or video by pressing the modify icon and then utilizing editing options like Filters, Adjust, Crop, Rotate, Markup, and Export.

You may also use the Google Assistant to send a photo or a video by asking the Google Assistant to do so, such as "OK Google, send a photo to Jude, saying I'm at the park."

Google Chrome: How to Use It

Google Chrome is your Pixel 8 Pro's web browser, where you can surf the web, search the internet, bookmark your favorite sites, and sync your data between devices. With the power of Google AI and the Google Chrome OS, Google Chrome is more than just a web browser; it is your personal online assistant that can help you discover what you need, remain safe and secure, and enjoy the best of the web.

To utilize Google Chrome, you must first learn the following:

How to launch Google Chrome:

To open Google Chrome, press on the Chrome symbol on the home screen or app drawer, or say "OK Google, open Chrome" to the Google Assistant, or squeeze the bottom half of your phone and say "open Chrome."

How to use the web:

To use the web, type the web URL or search query in the address bar at the top of the screen, then hit the Go icon or Enter key.

You may also explore the web by pressing on the Tab symbol at the bottom of the screen and then selecting the tab from the list of open tabs. You may also explore the web by pressing on the Menu symbol in the upper right corner of the screen and then selecting an option, such as the New tab, Incognito tab, Bookmarks, History, or Downloads.

How to search the internet:

You can search the internet using Google Search, which is integrated with Google Chrome and allows you to search the web using your voice, camera, or keyboard, and includes features such as Google Lens, Google Voice Search, and Google Suggestions.

You may search the internet by pressing on the Microphone or Lens symbol to the right of the address bar, voicing your question or scanning an item, or entering your query in the address bar and then hitting on the Go icon or Enter key.

How to search the internet:

You can search the internet by tapping on the Google icon in the bottom left corner of the screen, and then selecting the option that you want to search with, such as the Voice, the Lens, the Collections, or the Discover.

How to bookmark your favorite sites:

You can bookmark your favorite sites by tapping on the Star icon to the right of the address bar, when you are on the site that you want to bookmark, and then selecting the folder that you want to save the bookmark in.

You can also bookmark your favorite sites by tapping on the Menu icon in the top right corner of the screen, then on the Bookmarks option, and then on the Add bookmark icon in the top right corner of the screen, and then entering the name and web address of the site that you want to bookmark, and then selecting the folder to save the bookmark to, or by creating a new folder, or by tapping on the Save button.

How to Sync Your Data Between Devices:

Sign in to your Google account on Google Chrome to sync your data across devices, allowing you to access your bookmarks, history, passwords, preferences, and extensions on any device that has Google Chrome installed, using the same Google account.

Sign in to your Google account in Google Chrome by pressing on the Profile symbol in the upper right corner of the screen, then on the Sign in to Chrome option, and then entering your email and password, or by selecting an existing account, or by establishing a new account.

You can also sync your data across devices by tapping on the Menu icon in the top right corner of the screen, then Settings, then Sync and Google services, then sliding the switch next to Sync your Chrome data, and then selecting the data that you want to sync, or by tapping on the Manage sync option, and then selecting the data that you want to sync.

What is the Google Play Store?

The Google Play Store is your Pixel 8 Pro's app store, where you can download and update applications, games, books, movies, music, and other content from Google and other developers. With features like Google Play Protect, Google Play Pass, and Google Play Family Library, the Google Play shop is more than just an app shop; it is your personal app assistant that can help you find, play, and manage your applications.

Opening the Google Play Store:

You may open the Google Play Store by pressing on the Play Store icon on the home screen or in the app drawer, or by saying "OK Google, open Play Store" to the Google Assistant, or by squeezing the bottom half of your phone and saying "open Play Store."

How to download apps:

You can download apps by tapping on the Apps icon at the bottom of the screen and then selecting the category you want to see, such as the Top charts, Categories, Editors'

Choice, or For you, or by typing the app name or keyword in the search bar at the top of the screen and then tapping on the Search icon or Enter key.

You can also download apps by selecting the app from the list of available apps and then tapping on the Install button, or by tapping on the Buy button, if the app is not free, and then entering your payment method, or by selecting an existing payment method, or by tapping on the Subscribe button, if the app has a subscription option, and then entering your payment method, or by selecting an existing payment method.

You may also use the Google Assistant to download applications by asking "OK Google, download [app name]" or "OK

Google, buy [app name]" or "OK Google, subscribe to [app name]".

How to update apps:

You can update apps by tapping on the Menu icon in the top left corner of the screen, then My apps & games, and then the Update all button, or by tapping on the app that you want to update from the list of apps that have updates available, and then tapping on the Update button.

You may also update applications by enabling the Google Play Store's auto-update option, which allows you to update your apps automatically, whether you are connected to a Wi-Fi network or using mobile data, depending on your preferences.

You can enable auto-update by tapping on the Menu icon in the top left corner of the screen, then on the Settings option, then on the Auto-update apps option, and finally on the option that suits you, such as Over any network, Over Wi-Fi only, or Don't auto-update apps.

How to manage apps:

To manage apps, tap on the Menu icon in the top left corner of the screen, then My apps & games, and then the Installed tab, or the Library tab, or the Share tab, or the Beta tab, depending on what you want to do, such as uninstalling, reinstalling, sharing, or testing apps.

You can also manage apps by tapping on the app you want to manage from the list of installed apps, library apps, shared apps, or beta apps, and then tapping on the More icon at the top right corner of the screen, and then selecting an option, such as Uninstall, Open, Share, or Leave.

How to find more content:

You can find more content by tapping on the Games, Books, Movies & TV, or Music icons at the bottom of the screen, and then selecting the category that you want to see, such as the Top charts, Categories, Editors' Choice, or For you, or by typing the content name or keyword in the search bar at the top of the screen, and then tapping on the Search icon or the Enter key.

You can also find more content by tapping on the content you want to download from the list of available content, then tapping on the Install button, or the Buy button, or the Rent button, or the Subscribe button, depending on the type and price of the content.

You may also find additional material by asking "OK Google, download [content name]" or "OK Google, buy [content name]" or "OK Google, rent [content name]" or "OK Google, subscribe to [content name]" to the Google Assistant.

Chapter 3

Advanced Features

How to Make Use of Pixel-Only Features

With the power of Google AI and the Google Pixel OS, your Pixel 8 Pro includes several Pixel-exclusive features that you can utilize to improve your experience, convenience, and security.

This section will teach you how to use the Pixel-exclusive features listed below:

Call Screen:

Allows you to screen unfamiliar callers and block robocalls and spam calls without answering the phone.

Call Screen allows you to see who is calling and why, and then decide whether to respond, hang up, or report the call.

When you receive a call from an unknown number, you may utilize Call Screen by pressing on the Screen call button and then following the instructions on the screen.

You may also alter your preferences, voice, and contacts by navigating to the Google Phone app, clicking on the More symbol in the upper right corner of the screen, touching on Settings, and then tapping on Spam and Call Screen.

Now Playing,

a function that detects music playing around you and displays the song title and artist information on your lock screen or notification panel.

Now Playing allows you to find new music and add songs to your playlist without having to launch an app.

You may utilize Now Playing by activating the function on your phone, which will identify the songs that are playing around you and display the song details on your screen.

By pressing on the song details, you may also access further alternatives, such as accessing the Google Assistant, Google Search, or Google Play Music.

You may also enable or disable Now Playing by navigating to the Settings app, selecting Sound, then Now Playing, and then sliding the switch next to Show music on lock screen.

Live Caption:

a function that automatically captions media on your phone that is playing, such as videos, podcasts, or voice messages, with or without sound. Live Captioning allows you to view and listen to media without disturbing others, comprehend media in other languages, and access media in busy or calm locations.

Turning on Live Caption on your phone will automatically caption the media that is playing on your phone and display the subtitles on your screen. By touching on the caption box, you may also access other options such as enlarging, collapsing, dragging, or concealing the captions.

You can also toggle Live Caption on and off by heading to the Settings app, clicking on Sound, then Live Caption, and moving the switch next to Live Caption.

How to Make Use of Google Tensor G3's Features

With the capability of your phone's latest processor, the **Google Tensor G3**, you may use the various Google Tensor G3 capabilities on your Pixel 8 Pro to improve your performance, intellect, and creativity.

The **Google Tensor G3** is Google's first custom-built system on a chip (SoC) that provides faster and smarter computing, longer battery life, and increased security for your Pixel 8 Pro.

The Google Tensor G3 is built to tackle the most demanding tasks with simplicity and efficiency, such as Google Assistant, Google Camera, Google Photos, and Google Translate.

You will learn how to use the following Google Tensor G3 capabilities in this section:

Improved performance, which allows you to run numerous applications and games on your Pixel 8 Pro smoothly and fluidly without lagging or crashing.

You can take advantage of the increased performance to enjoy the most of Android 12 and the Pixel Launcher, including features like Material You, the Privacy Dashboard, and Quick Tap.

You may benefit from the increased performance by using your phone normally and noting the difference in speed and stability when compared to other phones.

You can also optimize your performance by going to the Settings app, tapping on Battery, then on Battery Saver, and sliding the switch to the on position to extend your battery life, or by tapping on Adaptive Battery, then on Adaptive Battery, and sliding the switch to the on position to limit the battery usage of apps you don't use frequently.

The increased AI capabilities feature on your Pixel 8 Pro allows you to leverage Google AI and machine learning to improve your experience, convenience, and security.

When compared to other phones, you may use the expanded AI capabilities to use the Google Assistant, Google Camera, Google Photos, and Google Translate with greater precision and efficiency.

You may take use of the improved AI capabilities by utilizing Google applications and services as normal and seeing the difference in quality and functionality when compared to competing phones.

You can also customize your AI capabilities by going to the Google app, tapping on the More icon in the bottom right corner of the screen, and then tapping on Settings, and then tapping on Google Assistant, or Google Lens, or Google Podcasts, or Google

Collections, where you can change your preferences, voice, routines, and devices.

You may use your phone to monitor your health and fitness, cook and bake, check the weather, or have fun with the new temperature sensor.

You can use the new temperature sensor by launching the Google Measure app on your phone, selecting the Temperature tab, pointing your phone towards the object to be measured, and viewing the temperature on your screen.

More settings are available by touching on the Settings icon in the upper right corner of the screen, where you may adjust the units, calibration, and feedback.

Using the Pixel Watch 2's Features

The Pixel Watch 2 is a Google AI-powered wristwatch that works in tandem with your Pixel 8 Pro and provides tailored assistance, safety features, and health information. With the power of Google Assistant, Google Fit, and Google Pay, the Pixel Watch 2 is more than just a wristwatch; it is your personal assistant that can help you remain connected, informed, and healthy.

How to connect your Pixel Watch 2 to your Pixel 8 Pro:

You can connect your Pixel Watch 2 to your Pixel 8 Pro using the Google Wear OS app, which allows you to set up and manage your wristwatch as well as access numerous settings and capabilities.

Follow these instructions to link your Pixel Watch 2 with your Pixel 8 Pro:

- From the Google Play Store, download and install the Google Wear OS software on your phone1.

- Press and hold the power button on your watch until you see the Google logo, then follow the on-screen prompts to select your language and agree the terms of service.

- On your phone, press the Start setup button, then press the name of your watch when it displays on the screen. If Bluetooth and Location are not currently enabled on your phone, you may need to enable them.

- Compare the codes that display on the screen on your phone and your watch, and if they match, hit Pair on your phone and Confirm on your watch.

- Sign in to your Google account on your phone, or select an existing account, and then follow the on-screen steps to complete the setup. Some services, such as Google Assistant, Google Pay, and Google Fit, may require you to provide permissions and enable them.

- Swipe up on your wrist to see your alerts, down to access your quick settings, left to see your tiles, right to see your Google

Assistant, and power button to see your applications.

Using Google Assistant on your Pixel Watch 2:

With the power of Google AI, you can use your voice, touch, or gesture to ask questions, conduct tasks, and manage your devices with the Google Assistant on your Pixel Watch 2.

To utilize Google Assistant on your Pixel Watch 2, do the following:

- To use your voice, press and hold the power button on your watch, or say "OK Google" or "Hey Google" to your watch when it is unlocked or on the always-on display, and then utter your question or command, such as "What's the weather today?" or "Set a timer for 10 minutes" or "Play some music".

- To use your touch, swipe right on your watch face, or tap on the Google Assistant icon on your watch face, if you have one, and then tap on the Microphone icon, and then speak your query or command, or tap on the Keyboard icon, and then type your query or command, or tap on the Suggestions icon, and then select a suggestion from the list, such as "Remind me to call mom" or "Show me my agenda".

- To utilize your gesture, double-touch the air above your watch, or flick your wrist towards you and then away from you, and then utter your question or command, or tap on the Microphone, Keyboard, or Suggestions icons, and then repeat the steps outlined above.

- Using Google Fit on your Pixel Watch 2: You may use Google Fit on your Pixel Watch 2 by downloading the Google Fit app, which allows you to measure your activity, heart rate, blood pressure, blood oxygen, sleep, and wellbeing using Google AI and the sensors on your watch.

To utilize Google Fit on your Pixel Watch 2, do the following:

- To monitor your activity, swipe left on your watch face, or hit the Google Fit symbol if you have one, and then select the activity you wish to track, such as Walking, Running, Cycling, or Swimming, and then tap the Start button.

By pressing on the Settings icon, you can also access more choices such as the Goal, Audio feedback, and Auto-pause.

- To track your heart rate, swipe left on your watch face, or hit the Google Fit symbol if you have one, and then swipe left until you see the Heart rate tile, and then tap the Measure button. More choices are available by touching on the History icon, which displays your heart rate patterns and insights.

- To track your blood pressure, swipe left on your watch face, or hit the Google Fit symbol if you have one, and then swipe left until you see the Blood pressure tile, and then push the Measure button. More choices are available by touching on the History icon, which displays your blood pressure patterns and insights.

- To track your blood oxygen levels, swipe left on your watch face, or press on the Google Fit symbol if you have one, and then scroll left until you see the Blood oxygen tile, and then tap on the Measure button. More choices are available by pressing on the History icon, which displays your blood oxygen trends and insights.

- Before going to bed, swipe left on your watch face or press on the Google Fit symbol on your watch face, if you have one, and then scroll left until you see the Sleep tile, and then tap on the Start button. More choices are available by pressing on the History icon, which displays your sleep trends and insights.

How to Make Use of Android 13's Features

Android 13 is the most recent version of Android, and it delivers new design, privacy settings, widgets, and other features to your Pixel 8 Pro. With the power of Google AI and the Google Tensor G3 processor, Android 13 is more than simply an update; it is your customized operating system that adapts to your tastes, habits, and requirements.

To use the Android 13 features, you must first understand the following:

How to utilize the new design:

Android 13 introduces Material You, a new design language that lets you to personalize the appearance and feel of your phone with dynamic colors, shapes, and animations. You may utilize the new design in the following ways:

- To change your wallpaper, press and hold an empty space on your home screen, then tap Wallpaper & style, then select a wallpaper from the categories, such as My images, Curated culture, or For dark theme, and then touch Set wallpaper. More choices are available by pressing on the Custom style icon, where you may modify the color palette, icon form, typeface, and grid size.

- To change your theme, press and hold an empty space on your home screen, then touch on Wallpaper & Style, then tap on the Theme icon, then select a theme from the selections, such as Basic, Crayon, or Collage, and then tap on Apply.

More choices are available by tapping on the Custom theme icon, where you may alter the accent color, icon color, app shape, and app backdrop

.

- To change your animation, press and hold an empty area on your home screen, then touch on Wallpaper & Style, then tap on the Animation icon, then select an animation from the selections, such as Bounce, Wave, or Ripple, and then tap on Apply.

You may also access more settings by pressing on the Custom animation icon, where you can adjust the animation's speed, direction, and intensity.

- How to utilize the new privacy settings: With features like the Privacy Dashboard, App permissions, and Privacy indicators, Android 13 provides you greater control over your privacy and security.

You may access the new privacy options by doing the following actions:

- To access the Privacy Dashboard, head to the Settings app, touch on Privacy, and then press on Privacy Dashboard, where you can get an overview of the permissions that applications have accessed in the previous 24 hours, such as the Location, Camera, or Microphone, as well as how frequently they have accessed them.

You can also press on a permission to get additional data, such as the app name, length, and frequency of access, and revoke or give the permission to the app by hitting the Manage permission icon.

- To access the App permissions, go to the Settings app, then Apps, then the app you wish to control, then Permissions, where you can see a list of rights that the app has sought, such as Contacts, Storage, or Phone, and whether they are granted or refused.

You may also modify the status of a permission, such as Allow all the time, Allow just when using the app, Ask every time, or Deny.

- To access the Privacy indicators, go to the Settings app, tap on Privacy, and then tap on Privacy indicators, where you can turn on or off the privacy indicators, which are the green dots that appear in the top right corner of your screen when an app is using your camera or microphone.

When the privacy indication shows, you may press it to see which app is using your camera or microphone, and you can also stop the app from using them by hitting the Stop button.

- How to utilize the new widgets: Android 13 provides new widgets that make it easier and faster to access your favorite apps and services, with greater customization and functionality. You may use the new widgets by doing the following actions:

- To add a widget, press and hold on an empty space on your home screen, then tap on Widgets, then select the widget from the list of available widgets, such as the Clock, Calendar, or Weather, and then drag and drop it to the desired location on your home screen. You may also resize or delete the widget by pressing and holding it and then dragging the handles or selecting the options that display on the screen.

- To personalize a widget, press and hold on the widget you want to alter the settings of, and then touch on the Settings icon, if it displays, and then adjust the widget's settings, such as the color, size, content, or action, depending on the widget.

You may also access other options by pressing on the other icon, which displays if it is there, such as Refresh, Share, or Remove.

Chapter 4

How to Personalize the Pixel 8 Pro

Your Pixel 8 Pro is a powerful and attractive gadget that you can personalize to fit your personality, mood, and demands. You may personalize your Pixel 8 Pro by changing the wallpaper, theme, icons, text, sound, and vibration.

The following are the steps for customizing your Pixel 8 Pro:

- To change your wallpaper, press and hold an empty space on your home screen, then tap Wallpaper & style, then select a wallpaper from the categories, such as My images, Curated culture, or For dark theme, and then touch Set wallpaper.

More choices are available by pressing on the Custom style icon, where you may modify the color palette, icon form, typeface, and grid size.

- To change your theme, press and hold an empty space on your home screen, then touch on Wallpaper & Style, then tap on the Theme icon, then select a theme from the selections, such as Basic, Crayon, or Collage, and then tap on Apply.
Other choices are available by tapping on the Custom theme icon, where you may alter the accent color, icon color, app shape, and app backdrop.

- To change your icons, press and hold an empty area on your home screen, then touch on Wallpaper & Style, then tap on the Icons icon, then select an icon pack from the selections, such as System icons, Pixel icons, or Adaptive icons, and then tap on Apply.

More icon packs may be downloaded from the Google Play Store and then applied from the same menu.

- To change your font, press and hold on an empty area on your home screen, then touch on Wallpaper & Style, then tap on the Font icon, then select a font from the alternatives, such as Default, Noto Sans, or Roboto, and then tap on Apply.

More typefaces may be downloaded from the Google Play Store and then applied from the same menu.

- To change your sound, open the Settings app and select Sound, then select the item you wish to alter, such as Volume, Ringtone, Notification sound, Media sound, Alarm sound, or Do not disturb mode.

You may also access more choices by selecting Advanced, where you can modify the Sound enhancement, Sound quality and effects, Dial pad tones, Screen locking noises, Charging sounds, and Touch sounds.

- To change your vibration, open the Settings app, tap on Sound, and then tap on the Vibration option, where you can slide the switch to turn the vibration on or off, or tap on the Vibration intensity option, where you can adjust the intensity of the vibration for the Ring, Notification, and Touch.

You can also get more options by pressing on the Advanced option, which allows you to adjust the Vibration pattern, Haptic feedback, and System navigation.

How to Change the Display Options

Your Pixel 8 Pro includes a gorgeous 6.7-inch OLED display with features including brightness, adaptive brightness, dark mode, color mode, refresh rate, and screen timeout for a smooth and immersive viewing experience.

Change your Pixel 8 Pro's display settings by performing the following:

- To change the brightness, swipe down from the top of your screen, then down again to view more options, and then drag the brightness bar to the left or right to make your screen brighter or darker.

You can also access more settings by pressing on the Settings icon in the upper right corner of the screen, then Display, then Brightness level, where you may move the brightness bar to the left or right, or tap on the Auto symbol, to switch on or off adaptive brightness.

- To change the adaptive brightness, open the Settings app, tap on Display, and then touch on Adaptive brightness, where you can flip the slider to turn on or off the adaptive brightness, which automatically changes your screen brightness based on ambient light and your preferences.

You may also select the Advanced option to change the brightness boost, which momentarily enhances the brightness of your screen when you are in direct sunlight, or the night light, which suppresses the blue light from your screen at night to help you sleep better.

- Swipe down from the top of your screen to view more options, then touch on the Dark theme icon to turn on or off the dark mode, which turns the background color of your screen and select applications to black to save power and minimize eye strain.

You can also access more options by tapping on the Settings icon in the top right corner of the screen, then on Display, and then on Dark theme, where you can slide the switch to turn on or off the dark mode, or tap on the Schedule option, to set a time or a sunrise/sunset schedule for the dark mode.

You may also choose the Advanced option, from which you can select a color space, such as sRGB, P3, or Display P3, which modifies the color gamut of your screen to fit the color profile of the material that you are viewing.

- To change the refresh rate, open the Settings app, tap on Display, and then Smooth display, where you can slide the switch to turn on or off the smooth display, which automatically adjusts your screen refresh rate from 60Hz to 120Hz, depending on the content you're viewing, to make your screen smoother and more responsive.

You can also select the Advanced option, where you can toggle the switch to turn on or off the force 120Hz, which forces your screen refresh rate to stay at 120Hz regardless of the content you're viewing, to make your screen smoother and more consistent, but at the expense of increased battery consumption.

- To change the screen timeout, go to the Settings app, tap on Display, and then tap on Screen timeout, where you can select a screen timeout from the options, such as 15 seconds, 30 seconds, 1 minute, 2 minutes, 5 minutes, 10 minutes, or 30 minutes, which changes the amount of time your phone's screen remains on before turning off when you are not using it.

You can also touch on the Keep screen on while charging option to flip the switch on or off, which keeps your screen from shutting off when your phone is plugged in, making your phone simpler to use while charging.

How to Change Sound Settings

With features like stereo speakers, an earpiece, a microphone, and a headphone port, your Pixel 8 Pro boasts a high-quality sound system that provides a crisp and immersive audio experience.

You may change your Pixel 8 Pro's sound settings by performing the following:

- To change the volume, hit the volume up or down button on the right side of your phone to increase or decrease the volume of the presently playing sound, such as the ringtone, notification sound, media sound, or alarm sound.

More choices are also available by touching on the volume symbol on the screen, where you may drag the volume bar to the left or right, or tap on the mute icon, to mute or unmute the sound.

You can also tap on the Settings icon to adjust the volume of each sound category, such as the Ring, Notification, Media, or Alarm, or turn on or off the Live caption option, which automatically captions the media that is playing on your phone, with or without sound.

- To change your ringtone, open the Settings app, then touch on Sound, then Phone ringtone, where you can select a ringtone from the options, such as Pixel sounds, My sounds, or None, and then press on Save.

138

More possibilities are available by pressing on the Add ringtone icon, where you may add a ringtone from your phone's storage, Google Drive, or Google Play Music.

- To change your notification sound, open the Settings app, then touch on Sound, then Default notification sound, where you may select a notification sound from the options, such as Pixel sounds, My sounds, or None, and then press on Save.

More options are available by pressing on the Add notification sound icon, where you may add a notification sound from your phone's storage, Google Drive, or Google Play Music.

- To modify the sound of your media, open the Settings app, tap on Sound, and then touch on Media volume, where you may drag the volume bar to the left or right to adjust the volume of the media on your phone, such as music, videos, or games.

More choices are available by pressing on the Settings icon, where you may alter the Sound enhancement, Sound quality and effects, Dolby Atmos, and Audio balance.

- To change the sound of your alarm, open the Clock app and touch on the Alarm tab, then press on the alarm you want to modify, and then tap on the Sound option, where you may select an alarm sound from the options, such as Pixel noises, My sounds, or None, and then tap on Save.

More alternatives are available by pressing on the Add alarm sound icon, where you may add an alarm sound from your phone's storage, Google Drive, or Google Play Music.

- To alter your do not disturb mode, open the Settings app and touch on Sound, then Do not disturb, where you can flip the switch to turn on or off the do not disturb mode, which silences all notifications, calls, and alarms except those you accept.

You can also access more options by tapping on the Schedule option, which allows you to set a time or an event schedule for the do not disturb mode, or tapping on the People option, which allows you to allow or block calls and messages from specific contacts, or tapping on the Apps option, which allows you to allow or block notifications from specific apps, or tapping on the Sound & vibration option, which allows you to allow or block sounds and vibrations from specific sources, such as the Media, the Alarms,

How to Change Network Settings

With features like Wi-Fi, mobile data, hotspot, airplane mode, VPN, and NFC, your Pixel 8 Pro has a fast and dependable network system that provides a seamless and secure internet connection.

You may change your Pixel 8 Pro's network settings by performing the following:

To change the Wi-Fi settings.

- slide down from the top of your screen, then down again to view more options, and then press on the Wi-Fi symbol to switch on or off the Wi-Fi, which links your phone to the internet over a wireless network.

You can also access more options by tapping and holding on the **Wi-Fi icon**, where you can see a list of available Wi-Fi networks, and tapping on the network that you want to connect to, and entering the password, if necessary, or tapping on the Add network option, where you can manually add a Wi-Fi network by entering the network name, security type, and password, or tapping on the Settings icon, where you can adjust the Wi-Fi preferences, such as Wi-Fi scanning, Wi-Fi

To change the mobile data settings:

- slide down from the top of your screen, then down again to view more options, and then press on the Mobile data symbol to switch on or off the mobile data, which links your phone to the internet via a cellular network.

You can also access more options by tapping and holding on the Mobile data icon, where you can see a list of available mobile networks and tap on the one you want to use, or by tapping on the Settings icon, where you can adjust mobile data preferences such as Data usage, Data saver, Data roaming, and Network mode.

To alter the hotspot,

- slide down from the top of your screen, then scroll down again to view more choices, and then press on the Hotspot icon, which allows you to share your phone's internet connection with other devices through Wi-Fi, Bluetooth, or USB.

You can also access more options by tapping and holding on the Hotspot icon, where you can see a list of connected devices, and then tapping on the device you want to disconnect, or by tapping on the Settings icon, where you can change the hotspot preferences such as the Network name, Security, Password, and Timeout.

- Swipe down from the top of your screen, then swipe down again to see more options, and then tap on the Airplane mode icon to turn on or off the airplane mode, which disables your phone's wireless connections, such as Wi-Fi, mobile data, Bluetooth, and NFC, to comply with airline regulations or to save battery.

You can also access more settings by pressing and holding on the aircraft mode symbol, where you may allow or deactivate certain wireless connections, such as Wi-Fi,

Bluetooth, or NFC, while in aircraft mode by sliding the switch next to them.

To configure the VPN:

- open the Settings app, and then tap on Network & internet, and then tap on VPN, where you can see a list of available VPN services, and tap on the service that you want to use, and enter your username and password, if necessary, or tap on the Add VPN option, where you can manually add a VPN service by entering the name, the type, the server address, and the credentials, or tap on the Settings icon, where you can adjust the VPN preferences, such as

To change the NFC settings,

- open the Settings app and go to Connected devices, then Connection preferences, then NFC, where you can slide the switch to turn on or off the NFC, which allows you to exchange data with other devices or make payments by bringing your phone close to them.

You can also get more choices by tapping on the Settings button, where you may change your NFC preferences for applications like Android Beam, Tap and Pay, and Device admin.

How to adjust google settings

To change the security settings:

follow these steps1:.

1. Navigate to **Settings** and then to Security.

2. Tap **Screen lock** to select your unlock method, such as **PIN**, **Pattern**, **Password**, or **Swipe**.

3. Select **Pixel Imprint** to add or remove your fingerprints. Your fingerprint may be used to unlock

your phone, approve purchases, and sign in to apps.

4. Select **Face unlock** to enroll or remove your face data. You can unlock your phone, approve purchases, and sign in to applications using your face.

5. Select **Smart Lock** to keep your phone unlocked in specific instances, such as while it's on your person, in a secure location, or linked to a secure device.

6. Select **Encryption & credentials** to encrypt your phone data, manage trusted certificates, or set up a VPN profile

.

7. Tap **Find My Device** to enable or disable the option that allows you to locate, lock, or wipe a lost or stolen phone.

How to change the accessibility settings.
follow these steps1:

1. Navigate to **Settings** and then **Accessibility**.

2. Turn on or off the function that allows you to zoom in and out by triple-tapping the screen or using a magnifying button by touching on **Magnification**

3. Tap **TalkBack** to toggle the function that delivers verbal feedback for everything you do on your phone on or off.

4. Tap **subtitles** to enable or disable the function that shows subtitles for media with audio tracks.

5. Tap on **Live Transcribe** to enable or disable the function that transcribes voice and sound on your screen in real time.

6. Tap on **Sound Amplifier** to switch on or off the function that improves your phone's sound quality and clarity.

7. Select **Gesture Navigation** to customize how you wish to navigate your phone using gestures such as swiping from the screen's sides or bottom.

How to change the Google settings,

follow these steps:

1. Navigate to **Settings** and then to Google.

2. Select **Google Account** to control your personal information, privacy, security, and Google service choices.

3. Select **Google Assistant** to personalize your Google Assistant

settings, such as your voice, languages, routines, and devices.

4. Select **Google Photos** to configure your Google Photos options, which include backup and sync, storage, face grouping, and sharing.

5. Select **Google Backup** to backup your phone data to Google Drive, including applications, contacts, call history, messages, and images.

6. Tap on **Google One** to access your Google One membership, which provides you with additional storage, advantages, and Google support.

Chapter 5

Troubleshooting and support.

To fix common difficulties, try the following:

For battery drain issues:

- check the battery utilization of your apps, alter the brightness and timeout settings, disable the adaptive battery and battery saver functions, or calibrate your battery.
- You may also utilize Google's self-help route to resolve the issue.

To minimize overheating:

- stop using your phone while charging, shut non-essential apps, remove the case or cover, or switch off the phone for a few minutes.

- You may also see whether your phone has any physical damage or has been exposed to water, which might lead to overheating.

If your phone is freezing or crashing:

- you may forcibly restart it by pressing and holding the power and volume up buttons for 15 seconds.
- You may also delete the cache and data of the program that is causing the issue, as well as uninstall and reinstall it.
- If the problem persists, you may also upgrade your phone's firmware or conduct a factory reset.

To resolve connectivity issues, such as Wi-Fi, Bluetooth, or mobile data,

- toggle the function on and off, forget and rejoin the network or device, or reset the network settings.
- You may also check for any obstacles, interferences, or distance concerns that may be interfering with the signal. You may also utilize Google's self-help route to resolve the issue.

To resolve camera issues such as fuzzy photographs, blank screens, or error messages:

- clean the lens, restart the camera app, delete the camera app's cache and data, or update the camera app.

- You may also utilize Google's self-help route to resolve the issue.

To reset your Pixel 8 Pro, do the following: -

- To restart your phone, press and hold the power button, then hit Restart. This can aid in the resolution of small faults or malfunctions on your phone.

- To restart your phone, press and hold the power and volume up buttons for 15 seconds. This can assist in resolving problems when your phone is frozen or unresponsive.

- To enter safe mode, press and hold the power button, followed by Power off.

Then, to confirm, touch OK. This might assist you in troubleshooting whether an app is producing issues on your phone.

- You may leave safe mode by restarting your phone normally.

- To enter recovery mode, switch off your phone and then press and hold the power and volume down buttons until the Fastboot Mode screen appears.

- Then, using the volume controls, choose Recovery Mode and confirm by pressing the power button.

This can assist you in doing complex tasks such as deleting the cache partition or conducting a factory reset.

To factory reset your phone.

- Go to Settings > System > Reset options > Erase all data (factory reset).

- Then, to confirm, tap Erase all data and Erase all data again.

This can assist you in erasing all of your phone's data and settings and restoring it to its original condition.

You may also use Google's Update and Software Repair tool to restore your phone to the most recent Android version.

Contacting Google support

To contact Google support by phone, go through the following steps:

1. Launch a web browser and navigate to the [Google support page].

2. From the list, choose any Google product or service.

3. Select **Contact us** from the menu.

4. Submit a special issue-related subject.

5. Simply phone the hotline number under the contact option.

To contact Google support through chat, go through the following steps:

1. Launch the [Google One app] or visit the website on your PC

2. Select **Support** from the menu on the left.

3. At the top, select **Chat** as the method for requesting assistance.

4. Enter your question or problem, then click **Send**.

5. Wait for a response from a Google expert and then talk with them.

To contact Google support through email, do the following steps:

1. Launch the [Google One app] or visit the website on your PC.

2. Select **Support** from the menu on the left.

3. At the top, select **Email** as the method for requesting assistance.

4. Enter your name, email address, and question or concern in the form.

5. Click **Send** and wait for a response from a Google expert.

To contact Google support through the community, take these steps:

1. Launch any web browser and navigate to the [Google Help page].

2. Select a Google product or service from the drop-down menu.

3. Select **Community** from the drop-down menu.

4. Look through the current subjects or search for your concern or problem.

5. If you come across a pertinent issue, you may read the responses or post a response. If you can't find a suitable subject, you may start one by selecting the **New subject** button.

Made in the USA
Las Vegas, NV
23 December 2023